Expecting Something Else

PRAISE FOR *EXPECTING SOMETHING ELSE*

"'I could not possibly get what I wanted.' A.M. O'Malley's *Expecting Something Else* is an unflinching poetic excursion into the emotional lavish otherwise known as motherhood. In evocative, poignant prose and collage poems O'Malley details the winding path that familial relationships are likely to take when one is born into a world where 'even if mother is a bitch, / mother is the bread and butter.' So much of life is choice—and yet the most important things, of course, are decided for us, decided before we're even allowed to arrive into them. Taut and multi-layered, *Expecting Something Else* is a haunting collection by a poet capable of astonishment and aggrievement in the very same stanza. And as O'Malley makes clear, 'blasphemy is easy in love,' always. If you have a mother, if you have a family—or if you have neither of those things—this is a collection for you."
—Jeff Alessandrelli, author of *This Last Time Will be the First*

"In *Expecting Something Else*, A.M. O'Malley writes, 'Since 1979 and not before, I've been trying to find a place to lay out my treasures and admire them in peace.' Through the chaos of a childhood in which beds were couches or the back seats of cars, colored by a mother's toothless smile, O'Malley knife carves her treasures and disappointments into haunting prose poems and orb erasures. Expectations of normalcy be damned: this powerful collection illuminates a life eloped from, and in doing so, opens a window not only into a particular experience but into a human desire to reconcile past and present. *Expecting Something Else* made me want to capture my own story with such fierce grace—that's what I look for in a book, and what I've found here."
—Alexis Orgera, author of *How Like Foreign Objects*

Expecting Something Else

*   **   ***

A.M. O'Malley

This book published by University of Hell Press.
www.universityofhellpress.com

© 2016 A.M. O'Malley

Cover art by Burton Ford
burtonfordart.com

Book Layout and Cover Design by Olivia Croom
bit.ly/oliviacroom

ISBN 978-1-938753-18-3

for my mother

MOTHER LOVE

I have always lied to my mother.

I try to imagine

her hands

on my shoulders,

all the

mother you need.

feel that

certainty

In 1976 women were burning things
tuna casseroles Maidenform bras
their lips on roach clips I asked her
why she'd married him the answer
was something about beer in frosted
mugs older boys in high-waisted jeans
with trucks shorts so short that they
required constant extraction fishing in
tapered sunlight These answers rolled
between us clinking against our feet

*

You are always gone or going A refrain
from you *I am just leaving Just headed
out the door* I can hear things through
the phone line I know there is a
difference in the sound of keys being
set down and the sound of keys being
picked up Ice in a glass The clink of
empty tumblers Anyway it's too late
I'm here now out front I drove all
morning and a few nights away from
the sticky city of frozen pizzas in my
freezer I can see you're tired your eyes
are sliding away Here lie down next to
me Lie down I will cry you to sleep I'll
hang balloons while you're dreaming
and pop the balloons to wake you in
the morning For once

**

Fences are my favorite—mended or
not They rise up from the ground *the
planet close up is only the ground* Keep
me here

**

She's been dying for so long now
It's as if she isn't dying at all I should
call every Sunday When I was small
her black hair was something I wanted
She and I moved around kitchens in
the same way we both shooed people
out When I look down at my own
body it's her body looking up at me A
mother is hard to have Now it seems
we may only have twenty or possibly
thirty arguments left

***

What I really wanted was a jean jacket
with silver studs What I really wanted
was Pony Boy *Stay gold* What I really
wanted was to be older in the back of
someone's car The Baptists left a bag
of clothes on the stoop The jean jacket
you held up had puffed sleeves *wrong*
You took my picture in front of the
foam core door I could not possibly
get what I wanted

*

It rained on their wedding day
Valentine's Day She danced with her
father in the Elks Lodge She wore a
veil like the one from her First Holy
Communion scalloped around her
dark hair Rain on your wedding day
means good luck travel money tears

*

Eloping is to run away with a lover
or to run away with no destination in
mind

**

I eloped alone from a mobile home I
eloped from a wood paneled hallway
and a back bedroom with a queen
waterbed that belied the general tone
I eloped from Mom crying through
the paper walls I eloped from Step-
dad with hands Eloped from hot dog
eating contests I eloped from belly flop
contests I eloped from Kraft American
cheese slices folded into smaller
squares I eloped from Neapolitan ice
cream in boxes

**

she has read all the poetry

and expects

picture-book

rapturous

love   In fact mothers often feel

The baby looks like a stranger.

You don't love her automatically at all."

gap

between   mother
baby   *and*

'maternal instinct'

I dreamed I had a drink Just one sip
After all this time the sentiment was
just loss I have never been afraid of
shouting it's all the soft whispering and
eye contact that makes me squirm

**

My mother took a tab of acid before
she knew about the baby Then she
thought she was having a boy—she
dreamed of a tall dark-haired boy
Padraig would be my name his name
She had blue blankets for him / me
and a tiny baseball cap When I slid to
the earth two weeks late suddenly in
a rush and easy as a fish—I gleamed a
luminous pink My mother named me
after a Dead song *First one's named
sweet Ann Marie and she's my heart's
delight*

*

The field behind our house was filled
with Devil's Horns that would catch
bare feet The neighbor girl's mom
drank from tall plastic cups We put
on makeup and danced for her and
the boyfriend to Aerosmith's *Love
in an Elevator* I tried on sex with a
high ponytail and padded bra with
ears red and throbbing The smells
of a sleepover were liquored sweat
Menthol cigarettes pancakes and Juicy
Fruit gum

*

I asked her about the fire There was
soot still on the hem of her gown The
hotel window piled with wedding
gifts She had lain on the bed drunk
with her wedding There was a fire
somewhere down the hall and people
woke to thickened air I asked about
when he left her in the stairwell She
said *Everything cannot be terrific My
bridesmaids wore dusty rose bell sleeves
hair parted in the middle flowing down
like so many Virgin Marys* There is just
one photograph she is almost off the
frame but smiling with her eyes cast
on her hand in his hand

*

I've never been afraid of being hated
only of being loved I will give you
the leash to choke me but you should
know I was born with eyes that never
close

**

I left behind foil packets of Oriental
flavor my mother's long hair cassette
tapes of Bonnie Raitt and Vanilla Ice
a pan of boiled eggs pulsing with
maggots tucked under the porch for
forgetting secret maps drawn inside
all of the closets I left behind crawling
into the kitchen cupboards I left
behind being small and I left behind
being quiet I left behind Christmas
morning Easter morning chocolate
sheet cakes and balloons *Happy
Birthday Ann*

**

My mother dug a garden with a shovel
three days after I was born We were
on a Greyhound headed to Colorado
before anything could grow I sat on
the floor and watched her put blush
only on her cheekbones I watched the
special way she looked in the mirror
when she tried on clothes Her mirror
face was serious sucked in cheeks
She kept the tags tucked into a white
blouse when we got our pictures taken
at Penney's so she could return it after
She never wore lipstick She listened
to music late at night and cried down
the tunnel hallway in her own slowly
leaking waterbed

***

At home I was rarely hungry At home
it seemed that our dogs were always
dying from parvo outside cats crushed
under trucks At home the ducks we'd
incubated flew away At home the
linoleum warped and peeled so we
taped it down and stood on that spot
when people came over My favorite
red dress had blue flowers and a
crooked yoke neck collar Ignoring
things is sometimes the best option

*

I always let my polish chip My teeth
are small in my mouth I used to get
sciatica Since 1979 and not before I've
been trying to find a place to lay out
my treasures and admire them in peace

**

I am still guilty for

side flailing at

mother

-the darker

that

ferocity.
we do not know how

to lose.

The young girl

wants what

mother has.

step aside   give

It has nothing to do with
logic.

I was hit by a car in the crossing I kept
eloping I eloped to nine western states
I loped in circles in cars with boys with
a Rottweiler named Peace I loped
along with Nine Inch Nails Loped
under sand dunes with psychedelic
mushroom trips in pup tents and back-
rub trains with men who looked like
someone's dad I eloped into tattoo
parlors I took off my shirt and had
black ink imbedded under the surface
a message to swim up later

**

My mother has banana skin easily cut
and easily bruised She fell off the back
of a motorcycle once She heard the
echo of her head thudding against the
pavement *I'm hard headed* My mother
got in a fight in a honky-tonk bar she
bit down on a thumb almost taking it
off A gang of bikers beat her up for
snitching on a robbery they put her
bloody head under a hot faucet the
sound of running water One grizzled
old lady tried to steal my mother's
boots pulling on them while she
writhed in the tub My mother kept her
toes curled and kept her boots

***

If this were Big Sur in 1952 I'd meet
you by the surf tonight We could get
pulled out to sea Let the ocean teeth
sink in Do not say you'll do it and lie
I'm always looking for that

**

When I see a flat head I think of the
mother Where I come from there
are no fathers I think of your mother
What she was doing instead of picking
you up Rocking you cooing cupping
and shaping that head with a tiny
diamond glinting on her finger Was
she watching *One Life to Live* Doing
leg lifts in the bedroom Eight balls in
the bathroom I think of earlier you
I think of your baby body fontenelle
on your baby head your fat baby legs
pushing the blue sheets to the side of
your crib the summer heat bringing
baby sweat under your baby onesie the
empty room flattening you

*

A metal tray clattered to the floor
Breaking starts early The doctor
wore running shorts he moved too
fast pushed too hard broke a negligible
nose bone Brand new blood ran down
the blue length of his arm I was pulp-
faced with a bent-over ear a pugilist
fists up for mercy The effort of freeing
is brutal Our gore and cord connected
me to her to life support to each
other *Oh look A cauliflower ear* cried
Grammie Lorraine her hands flashing
with a camera The photographs from
that day are evidence with rounded
1970's corners They are scenes of
small feet and a flailing arm The
bloom of a minted mother can be seen
in the background

*

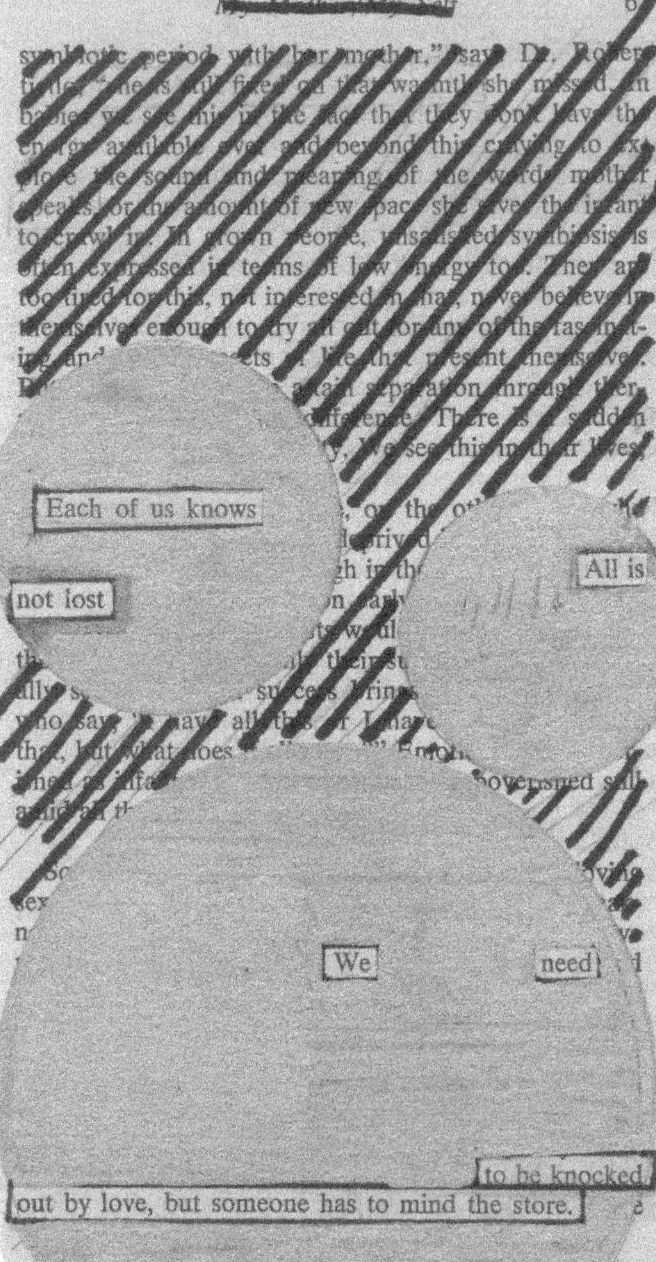
Each of us knows
not lost
All is
We
need
to be knocked
out by love, but someone has to mind the store.

I followed people home and cried
in their kitchens Drank sloe gin fizz
Woke up in vomit Woke up naked
woke up sore I rode in small spaces
Packed light I threw things away I
kept notes I burned notes I said I was
fifteen when I was twelve I said I was
eighteen when I was fifteen I kept
eloping

**

I'm still trying to find the right
combination of keys for this deadbolt I
listen for the tumble of locks I've seen
people die of weakness—look at them
I wish like the Gila monster we could
change with our surrenders I wish like
the dodo bird we could all disappear

**

She was a belled cat I lay awake in beds
full of other people's children waiting
for her to come home My mother took
me to the bar on Saturday afternoons
Tight Levi's and thin cotton shirts
were her uniform I waded the creek
out back with other wild kids we
dared each other to cross the rushing
water—I hadn't found anything to be
afraid of yet Later I would play pool
The jukebox—Cream The Flying
Burrito Brothers Pink Floyd I ate
peanuts to toss the shells on the floor
Those nights wore long I lay down in
a booth counting dollar bills on the
ceiling

***

She wanted me to arrive early She
wanted me to arrive the day my father
turned twenty-eight The brooms
of October were sweeping up as she
dialed his number The street lamps
coming on A cold wind whistle came
through a crack in the glass booth She
was crying in rhythm with the ringing
her best friend Diane outside looking
in eyes bright but mouth flat Both of
them drunk with the wildness of freed
animals It is sometimes impossible to
sober up She meant to say *I named her
after a Grateful Dead Song* but instead
started to sing He hung up to the
sound She looked up at Diane looked
down They doubled open mouthed
with mirth at the sight of wet circles
spreading across my mother's blouse

*

'Call me when you get there. Call me when you get there.

We don't want to be   our mother,
she was the victor."
                        we are thirty-three   whining
at our own husbands
we take   her voice   those expressions

          what became of the

                                        daughters of

A man named Tiny had a gold tooth
and wide motorcycle burns on his
calves I slept with him on a foam mat I
had sex with my boss Kenny on a table
in a glass office I had sex with a bald
Methodist minister named Larry who
sweat all over my chest I had sex with
my friend's ex-boyfriend in the back
of a dark bar—he wore a paisley shirt
I had sex with my first love in a gas
station bathroom while people knocked
on the door I had sex with Alice—we
wore the same bra I kept eloping

**

In the cold my hair goes brittle I pour oil onto it at night I'm not the one who saw Jesus in the toast I remember the smoke when John Paul II died If I could afford it I'd eat everything out of plastic tubs

**

Something happened to her front
tooth it was grey inside her smile She
never held her hand over it my mother
always smiled big My mother got her
front teeth pulled at age twenty-nine
She got dentures at thirty-two they
hurt her mouth too much to wear very
often She sighed with embarrassment
each time the Jehovah's Witnesses saw
her with her mouth sunken and slack

***

even if mother is a bitch,

mother is the bread and butter

Mother's brothers passed me like salt
Her sisters took me out of each other's
arms with fingers spread to protect
my neck Aunt Margie and Grammie
Lorraine prayed three rosaries for me
on the black rosary from Ireland that
hung beside the telephone in the hall
The same rosary that was draped on
my uncle Tommy's hands when he laid
dead in the front room For luck Aunt
Christie baptized me in the kitchen
sink when my fever spiked Blasphemy
is easy in love She anointed my head
with canola oil washed away my sins at
the tap Father O'Neil wouldn't baptize
a bastard baby and to make it worse
I was black haired with a rosebud
mouth Evil half-circle fingernails like
ice shavings *A devil in the cradle* he said

*

I made cold calls to sell Kirby vacuums
I took drink orders and brought the
salads out first *French Ranch Bleu Cheese
Thousand Island Raspberry Vinaigrette*
I could hold three pint glasses in
one hand Inspected dry cleaning
scraped at blood and semen with my
fingernail Worked in a shelter a call
center a library a bookstore Sold the
environment Sold human rights I
kept eloping I covered my arms with
long sleeves I cut my hair cropped my
shirts shortened my skirts I fluffed and
fought I kept eloping

**

A deer is something I have inside
my blood—I don't know what that
means—I've never been afraid of being
alone it's being held that scares me

**

it is a defeat to become your
mother.
If you
follow
out of a sense of inevitability.

Alternatives have come along
held great
exhilarating

danger.

for a time.

But I don't
belong
I'm just going to drift
away.

My mother can't stand the taste of
coconut even the smell makes her
sick She eats pickles with spaghetti
Parmesan from a can hamburger
patties on white bread with ketchup
salt and pepper on her pancakes Lots
of salt lots of butter My mother bakes
chicken until it is sawdust and slathers
it in BBQ sauce boils broccoli to mush
I tasted mayonnaise for the first time
at age twelve and hated her and hated
her and hated her Miracle Whip

***

To strike out on a new road
is difficult.

break from the girl that mother wanted us to be.

we will not be able to go back.

It wasn't so bad.

I let go of everything the way one
does on an airplane I sit down in a
good mood to try to be myself which
becomes impossible This one thing
could be true Truth even in just this
one thing To remember that I am
pure body I am butter on hot toast I
am scalded fingers holding dog-eared
paperback

**

The Good Christian Woman held me I
cried Together we went under the water
Her hair stayed on the surface like a
lily pad My eyes stayed open looking
for a face I was saved again The Good
Christian Woman painted one room
pearl with sponges of cotton candy
pink She stenciled a new name for me
on the wall I heard that name once spit
from Grammie Lorraine's mouth The
Good Christian Woman filed papers
She made plans ticked off lists on legal
sized pads My mother came out from
under her tree gave herself a birdbath
She held me for hour-long visits in the
Good Christian Woman's yellow ranch
house Sang in a warbler voice *please
don't take my sunshine away*

*

Hey hey you Girl Come here, come here I
was called babe baby babygirl sweetie
sweetheart hon honey sugar pretty
lady pretty lady bitch stupid bitch
cunt fat cunt cutie whore fat whore
stupid whore fish taco girl girlie miss
missy ma'am madam freak she a freak
hey girl hey boo hey mama mommy
mamacita *You always do that You never
said that You never want to fuck What's
your name Mary Ann Mary Lou Sue
Ann Annie Anna Angie Amy AnnaLee
Come on AnnaLee, come here Have you
ever heard of Jungle Fever Hey, take a
ride on THIS Would you like some fries
with that shake? Dance with me DANCE
WITH ME COME ON COME ON
COME ON Can we get a smile Let's see
a smile dayumm damn damn Can I get
your number I like your eyes I like your
hair I like your style* I kept eloping

**

This reminds me of an important fact
Most people die of choking because
they leave the room where they die of
embarrassment

**

My mother was a welder She tied
herself to the outsides of buildings and
made arcs and sparks The men on the
job grabbed her ass and then tried to
kill her Dumping a wheelbarrow of
rebar on her head while she welded
ten stories up wasn't enough the
first time She fell five flights and
caught herself She came home on the
weekends I followed her from room
to room I stood outside the bathroom
door while she showered I wore her
leather apron I let it push me to the
floor like a soft paperweight

***

I am almost the next in line to die
after you after you after you We are all
standing in line Sometimes elegies just
don't work You died ten years ago you
died last week you called me yesterday
on your birthday I could have sworn
you were dead It is difficult to trust
poems they keep trying to tie ribbons
on to things

**

My mother slept under the eaves of a
blue spruce The boughs kept the bugs
out and the cool night in She washed
up pits and ass in the bathroom of a
tavern She wedged her head under
the hand sink She twined her hair
in ringlets around her fingers and
settled them on her shoulders Her left
heel had a hole in it but it was a hot
summer so she didn't care Under the
spruce boughs she dreamed the baby
was carried off by a pack of wolves
Drops of brown blood an empty
mitten left in a house with shotgun
stacks of rooms that she had to run
through to find me When she woke I
had always been gone for a while

*

anything

I've inherited from my mother.

is

a   triumph

I   long

to see

a day in her life,

Whether we want our mother's life or not,

We have

The smell of pot in our living room
was a secret that came from the coffee
table drawer I lay under the long low
table and drew a map on the underside
When she didn't come home there
was a Soft n' Dry smelling nightgown
Marlboros I tucked them under my
pillow Boyfriends got more upset
than I did Grateful Dead Broken glass
Slashed tires A rose sulking on its stem
I put a card in the spokes of my bike
I lay in the lawn and listened to her
sing when she returned She washed
the dishes and played the piano I was
there when she decided to get married
When she decided to quit When
she decided to have baby When she
decided to have another baby When
she decided to stay When she decided
to leave When she decided

*

Beds were couches foam mattresses
two inches alongside an AWOL soldier
in a twin bed I loped across fields in
bare feet with a stitch in my side Ate
peanut butter and apples for weeks I
made lefse in a borrowed kitchen The
backseats of cars became dangerous
I kept a fork in my bag I kept keys
between my fingers I kept eloping

**

'nice girls.'

see love and sex as opposites.

fervor

is fired with

confusion,

Believe that

Mother loves you best

offer   impossible love

real

love

perfect love

It is a bargain

My mother was a maid She had to
wear white for everyday and a bright
pink Mexican Fiesta dress for special
occasions I went with her and watched
the Mickey Mouse Club on a bearskin
rug I drank Tab from the can with a
bendable straw I helped her wash tiny
Pomeranians held their warm bodies
in towels rocked them like babies

***

It is true that the outside of my body
all of my body was once inside of your
body It is true that once you grew
me I'll never get that feeling again
Which is why I am here to revive
you you must be partly alive still
How long will you die How many times
do you need to die How many times will
you kill me with your inhalations and
exhalations You disappear and reappear
sometimes in the mirror sometimes
in my feet always in my hands with
their leftedness and their veins I am
now resisting this as an epitaph I
am resisting resolution Let's leave it
unclear

**

the promise of

mother

Early on,

splitting

us.

convinced

us,

that

We

good mother.

had a

Grammie Lorraine became a bundle
of kindling Veins wrapped her up like
cordwood Her long hands narrow and
nicotine stained—remain un-inherited
Potato salad for thirty-five people
She slid off off her thin gold wedding
band The mother's ring with ten small
stones She stirred radish boiled eggs
cubed potatoes celery and onion with
those thin hands Bits of yellow yolk
clung to her fingers like children as
she tumbled a vat of salad Grammie
Lorraine wiped and wiped the counter
tops floors asses with long hands She
hung wallpaper mowed the lawn drank
Folgers coffee with Sweet-n-Low and
Coffee Mate Non-Dairy Creamer She
smoked cigarettes ruthlessly blazing
through pack after pack Grammie
Lorraine saw me first she called me
cauliflower She knew the name of the
moon and gave it to me

*

I learned to crawl home There was a
chimney fire an electrical fire There
were fights that no one could have
broken up Blackouts Black eyes
Overcast rainstorms lightning struck
There were broken bones hangnails
People died some quickly some slowly
I went to funerals weddings I kept
eloping

**

I was a baby I grew up in the back seat
of a car Most girls remember their
childhood bedrooms like I remember
tears in upholstery smells changing
from rusty to mossy in April Distorted
radio August then November Thin air
deep snow The lung-stinging winters
that give way to foxglove punctuated
by the sharp smell of dairy cow
Molasses-thick waves of black flies
Broiling stillness too The Saguaro
cacti stood out against the desert Mom
tried to start the 1978 Dodge Colt
with a screwdriver The tape deck had
one cassette stuck inside *The Sound of
Music* At last the engine caught fire in
a grocery store parking lot

*

Difficulties begin with the word *love*

'I love you,   mother says

                    but

            Often it is not love,

                    down deep we feel

it.

            "Love is

a   big package

            we did not get

I threw a phone at her head My
mother slammed her fist into my
bedroom wall and made a hole My
mother drove too fast when she was
angry I screamed, *I hate you* She hung a
plastic bag with a box of condoms and
a Wonderbra on my bedroom door
My mother said she'd rather I had sex
at home than in a car She made me
pour twenty-four cans of Busch Lite
into the toilet while she smoked in the
tub I wrote in my diary that I hated
her that she was a selfish fucking bitch
then I locked it shut and hid it under
my mattress—she wrote in the margin
that I didn't understand what she was
going through

***

A meeting of Alcoholics Anonymous
was not necessarily a playground
In those haze hatted rooms drunks
cried and smoked I sat in the corner
kicking the wall wishing for a canopy
bed A man with horn rimmed glasses
anchors on his forearms like Popeye
with bald pate came from the room
and gave me a small hard-bound copy
of *The Red Pony* I wrote my name with
sloping letters in the inside cover but
didn't read the book until much later
It would be a long time before I found
out about the boy and his helpless
nursing of a doomed damp pony

*

We thought we didn't exist any more
but it was only the postman refusing
to deliver the mail

*

I learned to love watching my mother's
hands—tying my shoes drying me
after the bath pulling mittens on to
my small hands that matched her large
hands I learned to fight by watching
her scream I watched her strip naked
molten faced to prove she hadn't
stolen her boyfriend's wallet When the
wallet was found in the couch cushions
she laughed along

***

The truth is

It is better

to pretend that

reality

is

wish fulfillment.

We were all away for Easter Three
days before I waded through poison
ivy in the woods I was freckled with
welts when I heard the news I can't
remember what caused the fire The
smell of melted plastic toys and
waves of soot smoke water on the
walls marking time like rings in a tree
marking disaster and rescue I like to
keep the chimneys swept just in case
I've learned that chimney sweeps don't
sing and dance and will rarely shake
your hand There is no such thing as
luck

*

Hi Mama Oh she says *How are you Well,
I'm out here in the woods so that's good
Yes that's good Good I've decided not to
get a new liver I know Ma you told me
that already You know the hardest thing
about dying this way is how ugly I feel It's
an ugly death an orange death Isn't that a
part of life I don't know what to say Well I
just want to fall asleep and never wake up
I don't want to last in your memory as an
orange person You won't be in my memory
as an orange person Do you remember
that circus we went to in Prescott Valley
No which one I was traumatized What
happened I don't remember I was
TRAUMATIZED Ma what happened
The elephants the elephants were crying
and there was nothing I could do about it
Oh There was an elephant named Tracy
and she had a big tear rolling down her
face and I wanted to just take her home
so badly and I couldn't Oh Ma I've never
been back to the circus Ok well I gotta go
Oh ok Bye honey Ok bye Ma Ok honey
say hi to Burton Where is he He's asleep
Bye Ma Oh I'm going to hang up now Ma
Ok bye honey Bye Ma Ok Bye honey yeah*

***

My mother chopped wood three days
after her heart attack Now I talk to
her on the phone while she smokes
cigarettes under the bird feeders
she says that she can hear a pack of
wolves at night they are her friends
She says she's saving the pain pills for
the end She listens to pan flute and
Gregorian chants She smokes pot with
the younger Sam in the living room
She would rather he smoked at home
than in a car

***

a   lament

Forget that

or   admirable   mother

"bad" mother   the

relief.   with a sigh of

We must give up our

ideal

daughters

are still children   afraid to risk losing

Telling the truth is a test;
between two people.

I remember the taste of metal Crickets
complaining about the noise Twin
lights crested a hill down the road
The red Rambler's engine ticked on
the shoulder of the gravel I thought
I heard my leg break I thought we
hitched another ride I thought people
were laughing in the front seat The
windshield left blood on my lip

*

I like to pretend He collapsed in the
garage laid there for two days before
hypothermia and dehydration took
him He fell while trimming trees his
neck was broken instantly He choked
on the disgusting slop from the
pressure cooker his face turned blue
then purple then he fell to the ground
He overdosed on liters of cheap vodka
in his coffee and prescription pain
medications He had a seizure from
withdrawal Drowned in his own vomit
He stepped on a rusty nail let the
tetanus creep up his foot and lock his
jaw Stroke Heart Attack Cancer Fire
Drowning Car Accident Crushed Hit
Exposure When I was a young colt I
dreamed of grinding up glass to mix
into his dinner of scattering his limbs
across the four corners of the yard He
has recently become afraid that he'll
die alone

*

She called me *skinny Minnie shining
star pumpkin pie* My mother says she
is a wandering soul *I'm part gypsy*
She hates to hear her neighbors She
doesn't mind hauling water or feeding
a wood stove all night My mother says
slick as a glazed donut says *I have to drain
the radiator* says *serious as a heart attack*
says *borrow me some money shoulda
woulda coulda* she says *pisscuntscrew*

***

face to face with

Our mutual refusal to show our true selves,

we are both destroyed.

mothers,

daughters.

dying.

every

I called

thing I did 'love.'

and

love,

holds us in an iron grip.

The Boyfriends arrived in different
colors They were all the same in
Wrangler jeans and dark sunglasses
The Boyfriends knew I had her ear
They brought gifts of dollar bills
folded into bow ties tins of caramel
corn they taught me how to draw
mountains They took me to the
emergency room for wood ticks
Planted pansies and petunias with
me in the shade of the trailer The
Boyfriends smacked me for talking
too loud in the back seat They hid
chocolate eggs all over the house
melting in their foil wrappers
They had their own daughters The
Boyfriends stacked up in a woodpile
outside the back door They littered
the yard like engine blocks The
Boyfriends still send dolls at
Christmas They don't remember my
birthday

**

My mother laughs easy as if she is just
waiting to laugh Her laugh comes
in a long low wheeze with her eyes
squeezed tight her head tucked into
her chest tears in her eyes nicotine-
stained dentures large in her beautiful
mouth

***

I grew up in a house of women   the loss of

the father   had its advantages

                         and   Of course I

missed him.

                                                 I
learned   about love   in the

first years of my life.

                                                'My
mother'

                                                with   baby

I still see   at twenty

girl

                     all she had to offer was her
          sadness.

My mother's second husband sat with
Rosie all night after she'd had her pups
He dozed and Rosie overlaid one with
her big tired body The corpse was the
size of his hand a girl another shade of
Rosie's gold He dug a hole outside the
fence where the other dogs couldn't
get it The dirt came up in clumps
not far from thaw He humped at
the shovel with only the dead pup
with him His nose and ears were raw
with cold when he laid the dog in the
ground Rosie whined at him from the
other side of the fence It was still early
when he crawled into my mother's bed
she rolled and woke to him staring at
the ceiling with a tear rolling along
the crack beside his eye She told me
this later in a low voice The phone hot
against my cheek

*

I won a lip syncing contest in 1988
A long time ago a man ran my uncle
Timmy down My grandmother still
bakes him a cake every April Stranger
to tell the truth I am not really here
anyway

**

I was a cluster of cells a zygote a
would-be zeitgeist screwed into her
guts She had a tender mouth an eye
for Maiden's Blush A borrowed Dart
just the two of us There's always
someone who wants to unmanifest
things for unmarried girls I was
conjured on a Mississippi party barge
with Joe Cocker records and a raft of
Southern Comfort on the rocks I am
here to say forgetting is to gone-away
like caboose is to late-night train On
the phone the nurse said the clinic was
unmarked that she ought to look for
a yellow VW beetle Once I caught a
ladybug in my hands legs so small they
felt like whispers Maybe she pulled
in pulled off one mitten Maybe she
pressed the cigarette lighter wanting
smoke the burn of something sure
Hand on a Winston mind on her baby
brother The size of his pinkie when
he was born I don't know what she
said when she drove away My ears not
shelled enough to gather sounds of
that world

*

When I dream of my mother her
nightgown floats over my head like
an idea I jump to touch it I know it
will feel like silk but it wafts away out
of reach Her hair runs away too in a
wave I reach for popping the joint in
my shoulder my hands splayed Once
she asked for an impossible thing I
don't know how people forget *How
can anyone forget Could I if I tried hard
enough* I never tried at all

***

ACKNOWLEDGMENTS

I would like to thank the editors of *Poor Claudia: Phenome*, *Burnside Review*, *Nailed Magazine*, *Unshod Quills*, *Jerk Poet*, *The Newer York*, *Fog Machine*, and *Portland Review* for publishing poems found in this book.

I would also like to thank the many people who helped me bring this book into the world: my publishers, Greg Gerding and Eve Connell; my editor, John Barrios; my many amazing writer friends and comrades—too many to list. Big thanks to Justin Hocking, Carl Adamshick, The Thank You Writers, and B.T. Shaw for mentorship, tough love, and support. To the IPRC for all the bacon and inspiration. To Regional Arts and Culture Council and Mother Foucault's Bookshop for giving me time and space to finish this book. And the most thanks goes to my mom, Tracy, and to Burton; I love you always.

ABOUT THE AUTHOR

A.M. O'Malley lives in Portland, Oregon where she is the Executive Director of the Independent Publishing Resource Center. *Expecting Something Else* is her first full-length book of poems. Find more about her work at amomalley.com and iprc.org

by **Brian S. Ellis**
American Dust Revisited
Often Go Awry

by **Greg Gerding**
The Burning Album of Lame
Venue Voyeurisms: Bars of San Diego
Loser Makes Good: Selected Poems 1994
Piss Artist: Selected Poems 1995–1999
The Idiot Parade: Selected Poems
2000–2005

by **Lauren Gilmore**
Outdancing the Universe

by **Robert Duncan Gray**
Immaculate/The Rhododendron and
Camellia Year Book (1966)

by **Joseph Edwin Haeger**
Learn to Swim

by **Lindsey Kugler**
HERE.

by **Wryly T. McCutchen**
My Ugly and Other Love Snarls

by **Johnny No Bueno**
We Were Warriors

by **Stephen M. Park**
High & Dry
The Grass is Greener

by **Christine Rice**
Swarm Theory

by **Michael N. Thompson**
A Murder of Crows

by **Sarah Xerta**
Nothing to Do with Me

UNIVERSITY OF HELL PRESS

Denting the world with words,
one incendiary book at a time.

CPSIA information can be obtained
at www.ICGtesting.com
Printed in the USA
FSHW01n1458220918
52283FS